Jazz Piano Solos

by Jeff Novotny

The Uninformed Security Guard (2012)

Harold Brown (2016)

Variations on "Bye Bye Blackbird" (2011)

Staten House

The Uninformed Security Guard

Jeff Novotny

V.S.

V.S.

4

V.S.

8

Slower, then accel.

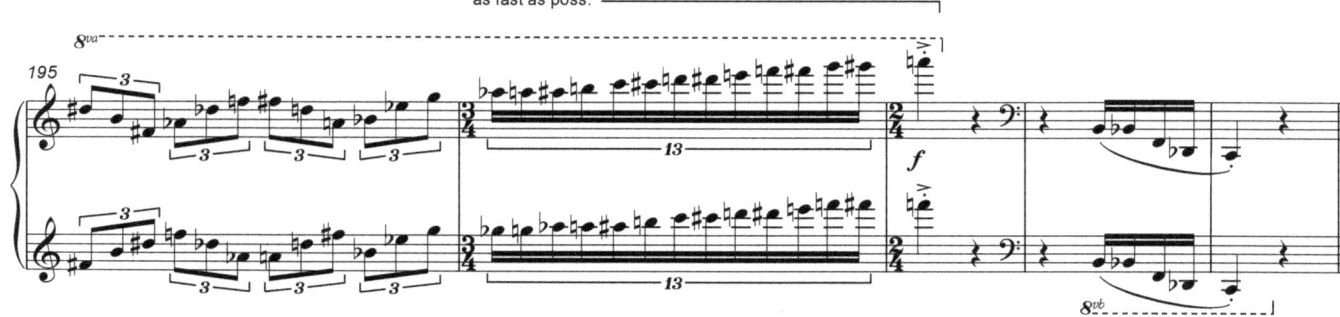

Harold Brown

Jeff Novotny

short   longer

Slightly slower, rubato; vary note
stresses ad lib. (quasi-ametrical)

Tempo I
resume swing feel

**Slightly faster,
str. 8ths**

No break
♩=180, swing

22

Andante   **Tempo I**

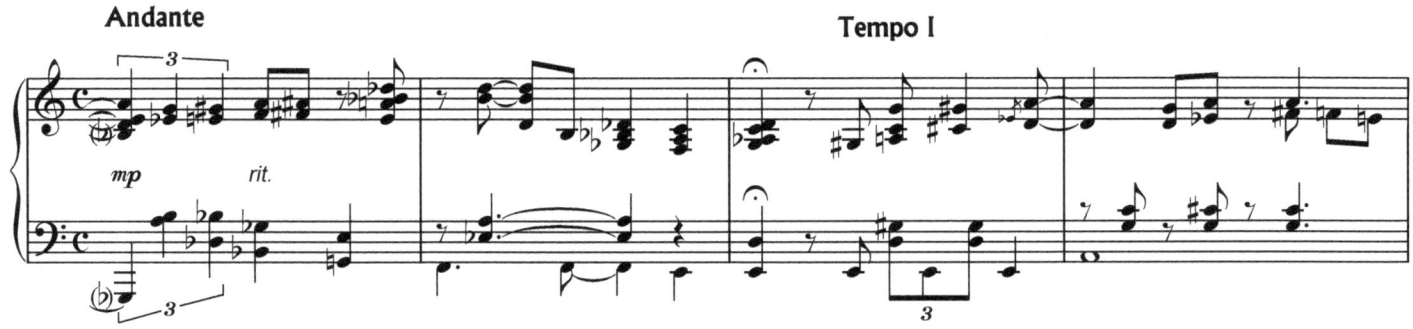

Variations on "Bye Bye Blackbird"

Ray Henderson
Arr. Jeff Novotny
As performed by Francis Hon

Dreamlike, mysterious
Molto rubato
♩ = 80

Tempo I